Underground
Adventure

Story by Mike Graf
Illustrations by Liz Alger

Rigby PM Collection and PM Plus
Sapphire Level 29

U.S. Edition © 2013 HMH Supplemental Publishers
10801 N. MoPac Expressway
Building #3
Austin, TX 78759
www.hmhsupplemental.com

Text © 2003 Cengage Learning Australia Pty Limited
Illustrations © 2003 Cengage Learning Australia Pty Limited
Originally published in Australia by Cengage Learning Australia

16   1957   16
4500630491

Text: Mike Graf
Illustrations: Liz Alger
Printed in China by 1010 Printing International Ltd

Underground Adventure
ISBN 978 0 75 786937 2

Contents

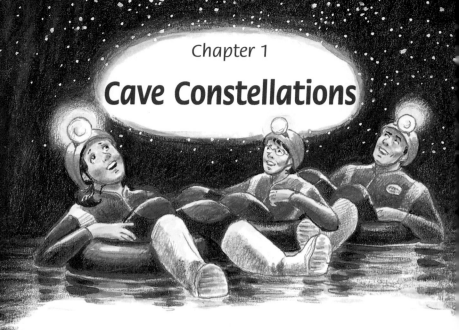

Chapter 1
Cave Constellations

"It's just like looking at the night sky!" Nina announced.

"Except I don't see the Southern Cross," Nina's father, Paul, said.

"Or Orion's Belt," her mom, Theresa, added.

"That's because," Nina went on, "they're cave constellations."

Nina's family and a group of other tourists floated through an underground stream. Two guides, Kelly and Rick, led their group.

"This is the 'Glowworm Cavern,'" Rick explained. "It's one of the largest rooms in this cave. And it's known, of course, for the glowworms that cling to the ceiling."

"They aren't really worms, though," Kelly added, "but the larvae stage of a small fly. Their tails light up by a process called bioluminescence. The light attracts bugs, which get caught in sticky threads spun by the glowworms. They eat the bugs."

Nina looked up at the thousands of tiny starlike dots of light. "Amazing!" she said.

"If you turn off your headlamps," Kelly told the group, "you'll really see how much light these glowworms can give out. Please be as quiet as you can. Noise disturbs them."

Nina and the others floated silently on inner tubes in the dark cave. Their wetsuits kept them warm in the cold water. Nina heard the others in the group but could only see their faint shadows.

"It's pretty great, isn't it, Mom?" asked Nina quietly.

"I've never seen anything like it."

"I'll never forget it," Nina said.

Nina rested her head back on the inner tube and stared up at the bluish lights. As she fluttered her hands through the cold water, she thought to herself, *I'm floating through a lost underground world. A world full of caverns, brilliant bugs, and ...*

SMACK!

Nina's tube bumped into a rock.

"Welcome to the end of the cavern!" said Kelly. One by one the cave visitors grouped together. Kelly turned on her headlamp and did a head count — "1, 2, 3, 4, 5, 6, 7, 8 ... Yep, we're all here."

"Everyone please turn your lights back on," Kelly asked. One by one the tourists flicked on their headlamps.

Kelly looked at the group. "This is an easy cave, but it gets a bit more difficult up ahead. There's a tricky spot about 15 yards around the bend. I'm going to check the water level there first. After a bit of rain it can be too dangerous. If the water is okay to go, I'll stay up there and wait for each of you to come through safely. Rick will give you instructions from here."

Kelly let the stream take her to a small bend, where she grabbed onto a rock. She shined her light around the corner. Then she turned and smiled at the waiting group. "This is the fun part."

Kelly let go of the rock. Immediately, the fast-flowing water whisked her out of sight. "Woohoo!" Her voice trailed off.

"I think you'll really enjoy this," Rick said while paddling to the front of the group.

"Hi, everyone!" Kelly appeared on a rock shelf far above. "The water level is up a bit, but it's safe to come through. If it were much higher, we would have to walk around this part. But then you'd miss out on all the fun. So, I'll be waiting for you."

Kelly climbed back over the rock and disappeared from view. In a moment, she yelled, "Ready!"

Chapter 2
Fast Water

"Okay, there is a stretch of fast water around the bend that leads to the big cave. Just hang onto your inner tubes, and enjoy the ride. Who'd like to be first?" asked Rick.

"I'll go," Nina replied.

"Cool," said Rick. "Kids are always the bravest."

Nina floated toward Rick, who then held her steady. She looked toward the narrow, rushing channel of water, then back at her parents. "I hope I see you again!"

Everyone laughed.

"Just wait for us up ahead," Nina's father smiled.

Rick pointed the way. "Once I let go, you will head toward that passage. Keep your feet up and your arms tucked in. Ready?"

Nina nodded.

Rick let Nina's tube float toward the channel. The rapid water pulled her along.

"Whoa!" Nina hollered as she disappeared around a corner. She bumped into a wall and spun around in a circle, then was pulled further downstream.

SLAM! Nina hit a rock, then stopped, then was off again.

"I'd take this over a video game any day, wouldn't you?" Kelly asked.

Nina looked at her guide. "That was fun!" she agreed.

"I'll let Rick know you're here." Kelly called out, "Number 1 okay!"

Nina's dad was next. Paul pushed his tube forward. "Well, here goes," he said, then plunged into the thin, narrow chute. "Ahh!" he screamed as the churning water whisked him along.

Paul bounced off the walls of the cave like a pinball. He twirled downstream then suddenly stopped.

He was wedged up against a rock. "Help!" he called out. Paul turned his tube until his feet touched the rocks. He pushed against the wall and thrust outward. The current drove him back into the same position. Paul pushed himself away from the wall again. He bounced off the other side and ended up right back at the same spot.

"Are you all right in there?" Kelly called back to Paul.

"Well, I'm kind of . . . stuck."

"Good one, Dad," Nina commented.

Kelly looked around the cave. Then she looked at Nina and pointed to a rock. "Hold on to this while I go back and help your dad."

Nina floated over and grabbed a rock bulging from the water. The current tugged at her, but she stayed in place.

"Are you sure you can hold on?" Kelly asked.

"I think so," Nina answered.

Kelly looked at Nina. "This stream takes us to the next cave room, so there's no danger, but please wait here. I'll be right back with your father."

Kelly flipped out of her tube, draped her arm over it, and swam back upstream.

Chapter 3
Swept Away

Nina held onto the rock and waited. She looked around the cave with her headlamp. There were long, thin formations dangling from the cave's ceiling that looked like giant straws. *Stalactites*, she remembered. Beneath several larger stalactites were stalagmites created by the drips from above. Tiny helictites jutted out of some of the cave's walls in various directions. The cave's ceiling sparkled with crystals. To Nina, it all seemed like a magnificent, underground palace.

Nina tried to switch hands so she could spin her tube around and see the other side of the cave, but her hand slipped off the rock. ZIP! In an instant she was grabbed by the current, pulled over the waterfall, and carried downstream.

Kelly held Paul's tube steady. He turned over and flipped into the water, then lifted his head up. "All clear," he said.

Paul grabbed his tube and swam with Kelly. They rounded the bend and looked straight ahead.

"Oh, no!" Kelly cried out.

"What?" Paul asked.

"This is where I left Nina."

Nina zoomed through rapids and over another small waterfall. The water carried her right toward a rock wall.

"Ahh!" Nina screamed. She put her feet out and instinctively covered her head. The stream pulled her into a passageway below the rock wall. The low ceiling of the cave whizzed right above her eyes.

SMACK! Nina's headlamp whacked against the cave's ceiling, knocking her light out. She sped along with the current and stayed low in her tube while putting her arms over her head and face.

BUMP ... SMACK ... Nina kept hitting the cave's ceiling. "Ow!" she called out. "Ouch!" "Ow!"

Suddenly, Nina slowed down. She lifted her arms and felt the air above her. The low ceiling was gone. Nina looked around and tried to figure out where she was. She noticed thousands of glowworms above.

Nina saw where the stream had rushed into a giant pool. She furiously paddled toward it. Nina grabbed onto a rock, ducked her head, and looked into the passage. It was tiny. There was no way she'd get back upstream. She drifted back to the center of the pool.

"Hello!" Nina shouted. "Can anyone hear me? Help!"

The glowworm lights looked like twinkling stars above. Tiny drips of water plopped into the pool. The water was clear and cold.

"HELP!" Nina screamed. "HELP!"

The glowworms dimmed their lights and the cave became darker.

Chapter 4

A Broken Headlamp

"That's right. She was right here," Kelly explained to Nina's parents — and the whole group. "But don't worry, she can't be far. I'm going to swim ahead."

Kelly flipped out of her tube and began swimming downstream. "Nina! Hey, Nina!" she called as she swam around a corner. "Can you hear me?"

Rick reassured Theresa and Paul. "She can't get lost — the stream splits up ahead, but rejoins the main channel at the next cave, where we were headed. We'll find her."

Nina floated in the pool. "Hello! Mom and Dad? Are you there? Hello! HELLO!"

She nudged up against some rocks. She grabbed on and stayed there. Nina held her hand in front of her face, but couldn't see it. She fumbled at her headlamp and tried to turn it on. CLICK. CLICK. CLICK. But no light came on.

Kelly swam around one bend, then another. "NINA! NINA!" she called out. She stopped at a small waterfall that plunged downstream into the cave's darkness.

"Nina! Are you down there?"

Nina took a deep breath and leaned back in her tube. *Here I am in this underground world with only an inner tube, a wetsuit, and a broken headlamp*, she thought. She lay still in her tube and began to shiver.

As she floated silently, tiny lights started slowly reappearing above. The glowworms were lighting up again.

Nina closed her eyes. Then she opened them, imagining she was looking up at thousands of stars. *I'm lost in space*, she thought. *Am I ever going to get out of here? Is this where I am going to die?*

"Hello! Nina! Can you hear me?" Kelly shined her headlamp down, then up, then all around. "NINA!"

Chapter 5

Not Quite Alone

Nina looked at all the glowworms. As she stared at them, they appeared to glow even brighter. Nina noticed more and more glow-worms throughout the cave. Some were even on the cave's walls.

Nina looked at the water and realized that the glowworms' lights were reflecting off the giant pool. The light of the worms and their reflection gave Nina a faint view of the huge room she was in.

Nina pushed herself away from the wall. She gently paddled her hands in the water until she came to the middle of the cave's pool. She looked up and whispered gratefully. "Hey, glowworms. Thanks for the light!"

Nina slowly spun herself in circles. Around and around she went. The gentle current in the pool pushed her back toward a rock wall. Nina held out her feet and let them hit the rocks.

"Whoa!" Nina held still.

Just a foot in front of her was an old wooden sign.

A way out, Nina said to herself. She started paddling. She rounded a bend and left the large room. Without the light from the glowworms, the cave became dark again. Soon, Nina was carried into a pitch–black chamber.

Nina was pulled along faster and faster. In the distance she heard the sound of water roaring.

For a second, Nina saw a bright light reflect off a cave wall.

ZOOM!

Nina was whipped further downstream. She slammed into some rocks, spun around, then stopped. Nina shook her head and blinked water out of her eyes. Then she looked up at a small waterfall. She couldn't believe it. Above the falls was a group of tourists. Their headlamps were moving in all directions.

Chapter 6
Glowworm Guides

"Nina! Can you hear us?" her father called out from the top of the falls.

"Nina! Where are you?" her mother hollered. "Nina!"

Nina looked up at the searchers and took a deep breath. "Here!" she called out.

The whole group turned to see Nina sitting calmly in the water below them.

Nina's parents scrambled down the rocks and helped her out of the water. "It is *so* good to see you!" all three said at once. "What happened?" asked Mom, as they hugged.

"I got carried away into a huge room," Nina said. "And I just came out over there." She pointed. "And my headlamp smashed into a rock."

Kelly smiled. "It's great to have you back. We've never lost anyone in this cave before. You must have gone down the smaller chute, to the big room in the cave we used to tour. How did you find your way out without a headlamp?"

"The glowworms," Nina replied. "Because of their lights, I was able to read a sign that pointed the way."

"Ah, the sign!" Kelly realized. "We closed that room off to protect the glowworms, but we left the sign in there for safety. Thank goodness the glowworms glow so bright!"